WORLD HISTORY

*The European
Colonization of Africa*

WORLD
HISTORY

Early River Civilizations

The Americas Before 1492

The European Exploration of America

The European Colonization of Africa

WORLD HISTORY: THE EUROPEAN COLONIZATION OF AFRICA

Library of Congress Cataloging-in-Publication Data

Nardo, Don, 1947-
 The European colonization of Africa / by Don Nardo.
    p. cm. -- (World history)
 Includes bibliographical references and index.
 ISBN 978-1-59935-142-1
 1. Africa--Colonization--History--Juvenile literature. 2.
Europe--Colonies--Africa--History--Juvenile literature. 3.
Colonies--Africa--History--Juvenile literature. 4.
Africa--History--Juvenile literature. I. Title.
 DT31.N35 2010
 325.6--dc22

                          2010008689

PRINTED IN THE UNITED STATES OF AMERICA
First Edition

Book cover and interior designed by:
Ed Morgan, navyblue design studio
Greensboro, NC

WORLD
HISTORY

THE EUROPEAN
COLONIZATION OF AFRICA

Dan Nardo

GREENSBORO, NORTH CAROLINA

Table of Contents

The Namib-Naukluft National Park in the Namib Desert in Namibia, in southwest Africa. The Namib-Naukluft is the largest game park in Africa and may be the world's oldest desert. Early European travelers were first attracted to the African continent because of its vast riches and beautiful scenery.

Chapter One:
Africa Before the European Onslaught

Europeans began exploring Africa's coasts in the late 1400s and early 1500s. From then on they vigorously exploited that continent and its peoples. Much of this exploitation was economic, though it was also often political and military. It continued off and on until the twentieth century, when most Africans finally gained their independence.

Europe's large-scale intervention in Africa, now widely seen as manipulative, even shameful, was not an isolated phenomenon. In that same era, a handful of rapidly developing, aggressive European nations reached outward across the globe. Spain, Portugal, France, England, Germany, the Netherlands, and a few others explored and colonized enormous portions of North and South America and Asia as well as Africa. Unable to resist the onslaught of more advanced, better organized armies and navies, local peoples everywhere knuckled under. And in this way, a few major, imperialistic (empire-building) powers steadily managed to reshape not only national boundaries but also the destiny of world order. As the renowned American historian W. H. McNeill put it:

Western European civilization, and [particularly] Western technology, rapidly increased the pressures Westerners were able to bring against the other peoples of the Earth. Indeed, world history since 1500 may be thought of as a race between the West's growing power to molest the rest of the world and the increasingly desperate efforts of other peoples to stave Westerners off.

Nowhere else was this race more pronounced than in Africa, and nowhere else were the consequences ultimately more tragic. As a result of the slave trade, economic exploitation, wars, and disease epidemics sparked by outsiders, tens of millions of Africans died before their societies gained self-rule. Even today, large portions of Africa still have not fully recovered from the ravages of prior centuries. As a result, many of modern Africa's troubles and struggles remain rooted in its past.

Greco-Roman Africa

When Europeans began exploring the interior of Africa in the 1800s, it became fashionable among Westerners to call it the "dark continent." The word *dark* was meant to emphasize that large parts of it were still unknown and mysterious to outsiders. On the contrary, however, Africa was actually not new to Europeans. Relations between Europe and Africa dated back to ancient times when Africa's northern rim became part of the European-Mediterranean sphere.

The earliest relations between North Africa and Europe developed in the second millennium BC (2000–1000 BC). Africa then boasted one of the most advanced civilizations on Earth—the powerful nation-state of Egypt, anchored on the Nile River in the continent's northeastern corner.

A map of Africa circa 1872

Egyptian armies often controlled Libya to the west, Nubia to the south, and Palestine to the east. Egypt had cities, writing, and literature, along with the largest man-made structures in the world—the great pyramid-tombs of the Egyptian pharaohs. At the time, Europe was far less advanced. The only sophisticated culture it had was centered on the large island of Crete, off the southeastern coast of Greece. There, a people now called the Minoans erected multi-storied palace centers and produced magnificent wall paintings. Although the Minoans—and later their conquerors, the Mycenaeans from mainland Greece—carried on a vigorous trade with the Egyptians for several centuries, the two continents remained largely separate; neither attempted to colonize or otherwise penetrate the other.

That relationship changed in the millennium that followed. The Minoan-Mycenaean culture gradually died out and was replaced by a people now known as the classical Greeks. Enterprising seafarers and colonizers, the Greeks built settlements on Mediterranean coasts far and wide. One establishment was at Cyrene, in Libya, founded in 631 BC. By this time Egyptian power was on the wane, and three centuries later a large Greek army commanded by the Macedonian king Alexander III (later called "the Great") seized control of Egypt. After Alexander's death, a Greek dynasty, the Ptolemies, ruled Egypt for three centuries, giving Europe its first major foothold in Africa.

Meanwhile, another powerful and aggressive European power was on the rise—that of Rome. Between 264 and 146 BC, the Romans fought three large-scale conflicts (The Punic Wars) against Carthage, a North African empire in what is now Tunisia. In the end, Rome completely destroyed Carthage and assumed power over large portions of North Africa. During these same years, the Romans had been conquering the Greek lands as well. And in the first century BC they took over Greek-ruled Egypt. At that point, according to the late historian Naphtali Lewis, "The entire Mediterranean Sea was a Roman lake and those who lived on and around it looked to Rome as the arbiter [decider] of their fortunes."

Despite their triumphs, the Romans controlled only a very small portion of the African continent. They and other Europeans were familiar only with the parts of Africa lying north of the vast Sahara desert, along with Egypt and to a lesser extent Nubia. The popular first-century AD Roman poet and humorist Juvenal summed up the Africa he and his countrymen knew, saying it stretched "from the surf-beaten ocean shores of Morocco east to the steamy Nile." For the most part, the huge areas lying farther south—the so-called interior of Africa—remained mysterious and spawned outlandish legends. Juvenal's contemporary, the great Roman naturalist and scholar Pliny the Elder, reported that the members of one sub-Saharan tribe were cave dwellers who lived on snake meat. "They have no voice but make a shrill noise, thus lacking any communication by speech." Other tribesmen had no heads, Pliny asserted. "Their mouth and eyes are attached to their chest."

Subhuman Desert Dwellers?

Like other Europeans of his time, the Roman scholar Pliny the Elder was largely ignorant of the nations and peoples who lived in and south of the Sahara. He passed on fantastic stories based on exaggerated or fabricated tales. About the Atlas tribe, a people who supposedly dwelled in the desert wastelands, he wrote:

> The Atlas tribe is primitive and subhuman, if we believe what we hear; they do not call each other by names. When they observe the rising and setting sun, they utter terrible curses against it, as the cause of disaster to themselves and their fields. Nor do they have dreams in their sleep like the rest of mankind.

Pliny the Elder, famous for his encyclopedic work *Natural History*, was a Roman scientist and scholar from Como, Italy.

The Spread of New Faiths

In the centuries that followed, the only Europeans and other outsiders who entered Africa's interior regions were scattered traders. Some of them doubled as missionaries whose major achievement was spreading new religious ideas among sub-Saharan Africans. Christianity was the first non-African faith to take hold; between the second and fourth centuries, it spread throughout the Roman Empire, including North Africa, and steadily made its way into Nubia. In 316 it reached Ethiopia, south of Nubia, after two Syrian-Greek Christians, Frumentius and Aedesius, were shipwrecked. They became courtiers in the royal court of Ethiopia and managed to convert the king to their faith.

For reasons that remain unclear, Christianity failed to penetrate in any significant way farther south. However, another fledgling faith, Islam, did. Founded by the prophet Mohammed (or Muhammad), Islam sprouted in Arabia in the early 600s.

An 1897 engraving of the exterior view of the Mosque of the Prophet, built in 622, Medina, Saudi Arabia

Travels with Muslim Merchants

Muslim merchants were more successful than their militant counterparts at spreading Islam across large reaches of Africa. The fourteenth-century Muslim scholar Ibn Battuta learned firsthand about these hardy travelers when he joined them in a trek across North Africa. He later wrote:

[I] pursued my journey, with a company of merchants from Tunis. On reaching Algiers, we halted outside the town for a few days.... Now one of the Tunisian merchants of our party had died leaving three thousand dinars of gold, which he had entrusted to a certain man of Algiers to deliver to his heirs at Tunis.... At Bijaya I fell ill of a fever, and one of my friends advised me to stay there till I recovered. But I refused, saying, "If God decrees my death, it shall be on the road with my face set toward Mecca."

After Mohammed died, groups of his followers began invading neighboring lands, where they vigorously promoted their new faith. They entered Egypt between 639 and 642, overran Tunisia (the former site of Carthage) in the 670s, and reached southern Spain by 711. Not all of the people in these North African lands converted right away, but over the course of a few generations most did.

Muslim traders also spread their faith, primarily in sub-Saharan Africa where they engaged in commerce. In most cases, only members of the ruling elite and well-to-do classes converted; the poorer peasants had less contact with the Muslim merchants and retained their traditional faiths, which featured the worship of nature spirits and the souls of ancestors.

An ancient Islamic mosque in Timbuktu, Mali, in west Africa

Many of the African rulers, government officials, and rich merchants and landowners who converted to Islam became enthusiastic supporters of the faith, often pouring money and energy into building mosques and other large-scale religious structures. These worship centers and gathering places not only served the needs of large numbers of people, but also increased the influence and prestige of local kingdoms. The mosques, as well as other religious sites and merchant gathering places, provided forums not only for worship, but also for education. Muslim rulers championed literature and learning, and the legendary trading center Timbuktu, for example, became the site of the first university in sub-Saharan Africa.

Medieval African Muslim ruler Mansa Musa exemplified this promotion of cultural advancement. At its height, his kingdom of Mali, centered mostly on the Niger River in west-central Africa, stretched for more than a thousand miles and had a population of many millions. Mansa and his nation grew rich from dynamic trade relations, especially in gold and salt, with most sectors of northern and eastern Africa and even parts of the Middle East. And he used this wealth to erect large mosques, establish a new university, and fund other large civic projects.

Mansa Musa wanted to trumpet his Kingdom's greatness to a wider world. At the same time, he desired to show his deep devotion to Islam by going on a hajj, or pilgrimage, to the holy Muslim city of Mecca, in Arabia. Surrounded by thousands of his subjects, he undertook the incredible 3,500-mile journey between 1324 and 1326. In the process, he made a name for himself across much of the known world, in part because of his charity: he handed out gold nuggets to thousands of people he met along the way.

A Cultural Isolation

Other Muslim rulers in north-central Africa displayed similar commitment to cultural endeavors and a strong devotion to Islam. However, their faith did not spread farther southward

A view from the third floor of Haram Mosque in Mecca, Saudi Arabia. Pilgrims face the Kaaba, the most sacred site in Islam.

into the large expanses of dense rain forests covering most of the continent's central portion. There, traditional African beliefs and ways prevailed well into the 1400s, 1500s, and in some places much later. For Europeans and other outsiders, these parts of Africa long remained untraveled.

Breakthrough developments in the face of this cultural isolation first occurred along the coasts, and it was the Portuguese who made the initial large-scale attempts to exploit the continent's least-known regions. In a sense they opened a door in which Europe forcefully and permanently planted its foot. And thereafter, Africa and its inhabitants were never the same.

Chapter Two:
The Coming of the Portuguese

It could be said that early modern European exploration of Africa was born in the dream of a Portuguese nobleman named Henry. The third son of King John I, who ascended Portugal's throne in 1385, Henry eventually came to be called Henry the Navigator on account of his fascination with ships and seafaring.

From an early age Henry was hugely impressed by two of the great realities of Portuguese life at the time. First, Portugal lay only a few miles north of Africa, which Europeans knew very little about and over which they had almost no control. Second, most Portuguese were devout Christians and either disliked or distrusted (or both) Muslims. Muslim rulers and their followers not only controlled most of North Africa, but also had a foothold in the Iberian Peninsula. As historian A. Adu Boahen explains, Henry dreamed of bringing Africa into the European fold and pushing the Muslims back:

> Henry's vision and purpose were to find out what
> lay beyond the Canary Islands [located south of

Portugal and along Africa's northwestern coast],
to capture the trans-Saharan trade, to investi-
gate the extent of Muslim power [in Africa], to
convert people to Christianity, and to form an
anti-Muslim alliance with any Christian ruler
who might be found. . . . With the financial and
moral support of the [Portuguese] Crown, Prince
Henry provided the essential impetus to the com-
mencement of overseas adventures.

Portugal's Advantages

Henry was no idle dreamer. In 1415 he persuaded his royal
father to send a military force to seize Ceuta, a Muslim
stronghold on the North African coast near Gibraltar. After
conquering Ceuta, the prince set up a school of navigation
in southern Portugal. There, shipbuilders, sailors, mapmak-
ers, and other skilled individuals trained with one major goal
in mind—to dominate overseas exploration, especially in
Africa. With regard to Africa specifically, Henry's purpose
was threefold: to explore its vast territory; to promote economic development and transcontinental trade; and to convert
people to Christianity. Additionally, he and other Portuguese
adventurers sought a faster, cheaper route to lucrative markets in the Far East, particularly in India. Existing trade routes,
running overland through the Middle East and Asia, were considered too long, difficult, and expensive.

Henry was convinced that Portugal would succeed in
Africa because his country was uniquely equipped to exploit
the continent. Robert W. July, a leading scholar of African history, clarifies this point:

[Portugal's] position in Iberia [directly in] the
path of the Islamic thrust into Europe had given
her a first-hand knowledge of the Muslim world,
an essential tool for [the] merchant-adventurer.

Moreover, Portugal was a nation of sailors; hence her people possessed the practical experience necessary for the marine [exploration] of the East which would eventually turn the African continent and outflank the established trade routes through the Mediterranean and across Asia. Finally, Portugal produced at this moment a royal leadership which combined ingenuity with stability, thus enabling a [relatively] poor and weak state to achieve successes seemingly beyond her reach.

July's point that Portugal was a nation of sailors is key. Not only did Portuguese seamen have the necessary experience, they also had the right ships. They were among the first Europeans to develop vessels capable of withstanding long ocean voyages. Chief among these ships was the caravel, which had not only standard square main sails, but also small triangular sails fore (front) and aft (rear) that allowed it to sail into the wind without the aid of oars.

An illustration of Henry the Navigator, reading a map and surrounded by supporters

Initial Exploration of Africa's Coasts

With these considerable advantages, Portuguese mariners struck out into the Atlantic Ocean and quickly accumulated an impressive series of accomplishments. They set up colonies and trading posts in the Azores, an island group lying due west of Portugal, in the early-to-mid-1400s.

They reached the island of Madeira, off Africa's northwestern coast, in 1418. And one of Henry's most capable pupils, Gil Eanes, sailed around Cape Bojador, on the northwestern African mainland, in 1434. Prior to this feat, legends had long circulated that a dangerous and impenetrable "Green Sea of Darkness" lay beyond that cape—Eanes demonstrated that this was sheer nonsense.

Eanes's voyage also opened the way for further exploration of the coasts in western Africa. Ten years later, in 1444, Portuguese navigator Dini Dias reached Cape Verde and the mouth of the Senegal River, in Africa's westernmost sector. The next major hurdle—the coast of Sierra Leone—was cleared in 1460, the same year that Henry the Navigator died. Ships from Portugal made it to the mouth of the Congo River in 1483. And a mere four years later, Portuguese navigator Bartholomew Dias made it around the Cape of Good Hope, on Africa's southern tip.

Portugal provided an excellent starting point for exploring Africa.

Western Africa's People and Plants

During their initial explorations of western Africa, Portuguese sailors observed the local geography, plants, and people of the areas they visited. This description of western Africa comes from the log of explorer Vasco da Gama:

The inhabitants of this country are tawny-colored [i.e., have brown skin]. Their food is confined to the flesh of seals, whales and gazelles, and the roots of herbs. They are dressed in skins, [and] are armed with poles of olive wood to which a horn, browned in the fire, is attached. Their numerous dogs resemble those of Portugal, and bark like them. The birds of the country, likewise, are the same as in Portugal. . . . The climate is healthy and temperate, and produces good herbage [crops and other plants].

Dias's accomplishment marked an important turning point. He and his immediate predecessors had shown that European ships could sail down the entire western African coast in only a few weeks. That gave the Portuguese realistic access to the Indian Ocean beyond. In 1497, five years after Italian mariner Christopher Columbus landed in the Americas, Portugal's Vasco da Gama reached what is now Kenya, on the eastern African coast, and sailed on to India.

Establishing trade relations with India was crucial to the Portuguese, yet so was gaining control of Africa's eastern coasts. There, Muslim Arab merchants had long enjoyed almost a monopoly in trade with local African rulers who, it was said, had access to rich gold and silver mines.

The Portuguese desired to wrest control of that profitable trade from the Arabs. As July puts it:

> Portugal, pursuing the expansionist dreams of Prince Henry, sought the double objective [of] throwing back Islam on behalf of Christ, while achieving economic ascendancy through control both of African gold and a sea route to the markets of the East. . . . It required only a few brief campaigns for Portugal to achieve her design of empire, [as] in 1507 Mozambique was annexed, eventually to become the central point of Portuguese authority in East Africa. A short decade after da Gama's first appearance, Portugal had become master of the coast.

Forts, Slaves, and Missionaries

The Portuguese were the first to admit that gaining control of Africa's coasts had been more difficult than they had anticipated. This was partly because they had sorely underestimated the skills and fortitude of their opponents. The European newcomers sometimes assumed that it was safe to go ashore unarmed because most Africans appeared primitive. One of Vasco da Gama's crewmen later described such a situation that occurred when their ship was approaching the Cape of Good Hope from the west in 1497:

> We were still at supper [when] shouts were heard [and] the captain-major [da Gama] rose at once, and so did we others, and we entered a sailing boat. The Negroes then began running along the beach, [and] they threw their assegais [spears], and wounded the captain-major and three or four others. All this happened because we [had] looked upon these people as men of little spirit,

Portuguese explorer Vasco da Gama, on his way East, refuses his crew's
pleas to return to Portugal in this hand-colored illustration.

quite incapable of violence, and had therefore
landed without first arming ourselves.

Such opposition proved common and formidable enough to
keep the Portuguese from venturing very far inland from the
coasts. Moreover, the explorers and traders did not feel com-
fortable building large settlements on the coasts—at the time,
it was far too expensive to send ample troops to guard such
communities properly. The solution to maintaining at least
minimal influence along the coasts was to build forts at stra-
tegic locations. The forts kept the explorers and traders safe
from hostile locals; they also served as collection and storage
centers for trade goods.

Among these goods were slaves that had been captured during raids of villages near Africa's western coasts. One of the
main targets was the so-called Slave Coast, lying due west of
the Niger River's delta. The first such raid, which took place in
1441, netted the Portuguese twelve captives, and by 1460 they
were collecting about five hundred each year. These slaves
ended up in Portugal and its eastern Atlantic island colonies,
where they became either household servants or agricultural
workers. At this stage, slaves were far less lucrative than items
such as gold and pepper. The scale of these operations was
tiny in comparison to both the ongoing trans-Saharan Muslim
slave trade and the enormous transatlantic slave trade that
would develop later.

An acacia tree in Mali, West Africa, on the Niger River coast

Successful Missionary Activities

Among the many early successes of the Portuguese in western Africa was their conversion of some of the Congolese to Christianity. In about 1485, missionaries from Portugal managed to convert the king of Congo, Nzinga Nkuwu. They also brought some of his subjects to Portugal to be educated. In 1490 King John of Portugal sent three ships loaded with missionaries to the Congo. They converted the rest of the local royal family, including Nzinga Mvemba, who ascended the Congolese throne in 1507 under the Christian name Affonso. He remained a committed Christian throughout his long reign (1507–1543). In addition to learning to read and write Portuguese, he built several churches and schools and created a new royal court modeled on that of the Portuguese monarchs in Lisbon.

Mounting Challenges

It is important to note that the Portuguese pursued starkly different policies in southern and eastern Africa than they did on the continent's western coasts. In fact they largely ignored southern Africa, a move that eventually would work to the advantage of other European powers.

In contrast, Portuguese traders and warships were unusually aggressive in eastern Africa. They pursued a harder line because over time the rich material resources of that region increasingly attracted strong and often hostile competitors and opponents. Among these were Muslim Arabs who were angry over Portugal's recent intrusion in the area.

Later, some of the Bantu-speaking people living along the eastern coasts offered resistance. In addition, both Turkish and Dutch traders and raiders launched offensives against Portugal's strongholds in the region. Faced with mounting challenges and setbacks, the Portuguese could not maintain their near monopoly of the African coastal trade. As a result, in the mid-sixteenth century a swarm of other European powers began moving in to compete for their own pieces of the African pie.

Chapter Three:
The Dutch and Other Europeans

Following the arrival of the Portuguese, the next major period of European exploitation of Africa lasted from about 1518 to 1700. More than any other factor, this era was characterized by a significant increase in the number of nations involved. Although only a few nations enjoyed widespread success, France, the Netherlands, England, Germany, Sweden, and others combined to shatter the near monopoly that Portugal had boasted. Those that were successful established economic, political, and to some degree ethnic presences in Africa that lasted well into the twentieth century.

Serious Competition

Of these enterprising countries, England was the first to encroach on Portugal's control of the western and eastern African coasts. In 1530 English explorer and trader William Hawkins began trading in what he and many other Europeans called Guinea. At the time this was a general name for the coastal regions of what are now Ghana, Benin (east of Ghana), and Nigeria. Another English trader, Thomas Wyndham, followed Hawkins in 1553. These expeditions sought gold, ivory, pepper, wax, and other valuable material commodities. But in 1562, Hawkins's son, John, began his own vigorous trading operations in the area and added African slaves to the list of goods. These operations created serious competition for Portuguese traders, who had been dealing with African nations for almost a century.

Guns vs. Bows and Arrows

An account penned in the late 1590s by English writer Richard Hakluyt recalled John Hawkins's second voyage to Africa, which took place in 1564. According to Hakluyt, Hawkins used early hand-held guns called arquebuses to frighten and capture Africans, who did their best to fight back with less effective weapons.

> [When] they came to a river [that] they could not pass over, they spied on the other side two men, who with their bows and arrows shot terribly at them. Whereupon [the English] discharged certain arquebuses . . . but the ignorant [Africans did not run] because they knew not the danger thereof, but used a marvelous crying [battle cry] in their fight, with leaping [about] that . . . was most strange to see and gave us great pleasure to behold.

Other Europeans quickly followed England's lead. The French began to arrive in the 1530s and sent expeditions as far south as Benin. The Dutch came later but proved to be far more ambitious and aggressive than either the English or French had been. Dutch traders, supported by well-armed soldiers, entered the lucrative Guinea trading corridor in 1593 and then moved on to the coasts of eastern Africa, where they brazenly attacked Portuguese forts. By 1607 they had severely damaged Portuguese naval power in the Indian Ocean.

Dutch forces quickly turned their attention back to the continent's western coast and in 1612 erected a large fort at Mouri, in Ghana. Not long afterward, they built two more fortified stations nearby and assaulted and captured several Portuguese strongholds in the region, including those at Elmina and Axim. Staggered by these blows, Portuguese traders were never able to regain their former power and influence in Ghana.

Emboldened by Dutch incursions into western Africa, the English and French began amplifying their own activities in Ghana. Their presence in the area had the effect of impeding Dutch momentum. The Dutch responded by refocusing their campaigns in regions farther south, around the Cape of Good Hope in South Africa, which the other Europeans had largely ignored.

The English, French, and Dutch were not the only outsiders to challenge Portugal's interests in eastern Africa. Arabs, Turks, and other Africans alike repeatedly attacked Portuguese forts on the coast; and by 1700, the Portuguese had been completely eliminated from eastern Africa north of the Ruvuma River.

European Limitations

During these economic and military struggles along Africa's coasts, none of the European powers showed any serious interest in the vast regions farther inland. Their lack of concern stemmed partly from an ignorance of what lay in the African interior. Furthermore, they had little, if any, interest in establishing permanent colonies in Africa. In one notable exception, the French attempted to set up a colony at the mouth of the Senegal River in 1687. Though the nearby peoples welcomed a trading partner, they were wary of having foreigners as permanent neighbors, and the French ultimately failed in this venture.

Giving up on colonization also meant abandoning attempts to introduce Christianity and Western education. Portugal experienced the greatest setback in this regard after it abolished its program of Christian conversion that had begun in the Congo in the late 1400s. Well-meaning and successful for a while, that effort eventually collapsed, in large part because of increasing greed, brutality, and unethical activities carried out by Portuguese and other European traders and missionaries. "The Portuguese Christianization of the Congo created something more than chaos," asserts noted historian Chancellor Williams.

> It was a revolting mess, no matter from what angle it is viewed. To begin with, priests were not the only [ones] among the leading slave traders, but they also owned slave ships to carry the "black cargoes" to distant lands. Priests also had their harems of black girls, some having as many as twenty each. They were called "house servants" by these "holy fathers." The great majority of the whites [including many missionaries] were the scum of the land from which they came. Even the half-educated priests were generally of the very lowest character, morally and otherwise. The slave situation became more and more desperate and out of hand as every white man down to the lowly worker became a trader. . . . One of the main attractions that drew thousands of white [male Europeans to western Africa] was their unlimited sexual freedom with all the black

An engraving (circa 1882) depicts African slaves in the Americas in 1619

girls and women who were enslaved and helpless in the power of their masters.

In spite of their failure to explore the interior, colonize, and spread Christianity, Europeans retained a strong presence on Africa's coasts through trade relations. The abundant supply of rich natural resources on the continent made trade highly profitable, and the industrious African people played a pivotal role in the business. Upon first encountering African societies, Europeans were often astounded at how organized and sophisticated they were. Many featured large towns with wide streets and well-built, well-kept houses comparable to average European homes.

Houses as in Holland

A Dutch trader who visited the main city in Benin in the 1600s was amazed that the houses there were equal in quality to most of those in Amsterdam. He later wrote:

When you go into [the city] you enter a great broad street, [which] seems to be seven or eight times broader than the [main street] in Amsterdam. . . . You see many other great streets on either side, [and] the houses in this town stand in good order, one close and evenly placed with its neighbor, just as the houses in Holland stand. . . . They have square rooms, sheltered by a roof that is open in the middle, where the rain, wind, and light come in. The people sleep and eat in these rooms, but they have other rooms for cooking and different purposes.

A sculpture of Jan van Riebeeck, a member of the Dutch East India
Company, at the National Museum of Culture in Pretoria, South Africa

The Dutch in South Africa

Although no effective European colonization in Africa took
place before the late 1600s, when serious settlement began it
quickly took firm root. Most of these hardy early settlers were
of Dutch descent. When competition with the English and
French in western Africa motivated Dutch traders to try their
luck in South Africa in the mid-1600s, colonization was not
part of the plan. In May 1652, the wealthy Dutch East India
Company sent about ninety men under the leadership of Jan
van Riebeeck to the southern African coast. There they established a small trading station. Their intent was to create a relay
point for the long journey from Europe to India and to allow
the Dutch to charge other nations a fee for using the facility.

Initially company authorities ordered van Riebeeck to
remain on the coast and to ignore vast inland territories.
Within a few years, however, the population of the station,
now the growing community of Cape Town, had significantly
increased. And a number of the residents felt they needed more

land for cattle and crops. So the authorities lifted restrictions and gave the farmers permission to settle inland. These farmers, whose Dutch ranks were reinforced with some French, German, Irish, and Scottish immigrants, rapidly spread inland. Collectively they created a society of white Africans—the Boers, or Afrikaners—who over time would come to dominate the continent's southern reaches. "Thus, the trekboer, or frontier farmer, came into being," Robert July explains.

> Moving eastward with his herds, he occupied territory over which [Dutch authorities] exercised only nominal control and he occupied it in great tracts of at least six thousand acres in order to sustain his cattle on the sparse prairie. In typical farming fashion, he had large families and each of his many sons in turn came to require his own six-thousand-acre homestead; hence, in only a few generations, a vast region had been swallowed up as the trekboers probed far to the east, well beyond the practical limits of the [Dutch] government.

Problems arose from settling inland in South Africa, the most grim of which was an increasing white supremacy. The Boers were strict, in some cases fanatical, Christians who saw themselves as a chosen people of God, like the Hebrews in the Old Testament. They also viewed black Africans as people whom God had damned. On the local, regional level, this triggered the beginning of the racist South African society that would later institute the brutal apartheid system in which whites and blacks were separated by law.

A Doctrine of Black Inferiority

Similar views of the superiority of whites over blacks had long existed to some degree along the coasts of western and eastern Africa. But by 1700 these views had congealed into a

A painting of Jan van Riebeeck after he landed in Cape Town, South Africa

deeply ingrained doctrine, or social principle, of black inferiority. Europe's exploitation of Africa was now widely and firmly entrenched. And one of its major dimensions was the ever-expanding slave trade, which was in large degree built on, as well as routinely justified by, that principle of black inferiority. In the decades to come, the insidious trade of humans would come to dominate European-African relations in ways that none of the earlier traders, white or black, had foreseen. As A. Adu Boahen put it:

> By [1700] there was hardly a coastal region of Africa in which the European nations were not operating . . . thus provoking deadly conflicts with the Africans. It is to the lasting shame of these European nations [that] they abandoned almost all the activities that would have benefited and improved the lot of the African . . . to concentrate on the most inhuman, the most destructive [activity, the] sale of man by man.

Chapter Four:

The Horrors of the Slave Trade

Slavery existed in ancient Africa—just as it did in nearly all other parts of the ancient world—and it remained a lucrative aspect of African trade in the medieval and early modern eras. The Portuguese began capturing slaves in the 1400s after they first landed on Africa's coasts, and other Europeans, including the English and French, soon followed suit and began acquiring black slaves, mainly from western Africa. The majority of these captives became laborers on plantations in the West Indies (the Caribbean islands), South America, and eventually the British North American colonies.

For a long time, however, the slave trade was a modest industry—the number of slaves taken by traders remained relatively small. It was not until the late 1600s and early 1700s that the transatlantic slave trade exploded in size and intensity. From then until the mid-1800s an estimated 10 to 20 million Africans were systematically uprooted from their homelands, and thousands of them died on the transport ships before reaching their destination.

A steel engraving (circa 1881) depicting enslaved Africans aboard a ship bound for the Americas

The impact of the slave trade on African societies was also profound, and incidentally, many western Africans became directly involved in the trade and increased their own slaving activities. People and communities suffered as a result of local population depletion, social disruptions, and political corruption. In the words of one modern scholar:

> The European concept of basing the entire agricultural economy of the New World on African slave labor proved to be devastating. Three centuries of ruthless traffic in millions of African men, women, and children unleashed an era of violence and instability in the interior of the continent. Many societies there fell into a long period of decline. Lamentably, later Europeans never imagined that African culture had ever been any different.

German philosopher Georg Wilhelm Hegel, whose ideas influenced nineteenth-century European thought, also advocated this view, saying, "nothing remotely human is to be found in the Negro character. Their condition is capable of neither development nor education. As we see them today, so they have always been."

The more deeply entrenched slavery became, the more prejudiced Europeans became toward Africans. For many Europeans the supposed inferiority of Africans justified a continued widening of the slave trade and exploitation of the African continent. A French aristocrat, Count Arthur de Gobineau, summed up in 1853 this self-perpetuating racist attitude. Black Africans represented the lowest of the races, he arrogantly stated. "The animal character, that appears in the shape of the pelvis, is stamped on the negro from birth, and foreshadows his destiny. His intellect will always move within a very narrow circle."

The Trans-Saharan Trade

The Atlantic trade was not the first African slave trade in which outsiders, including some Europeans, took part. Modern scholars believe that Muslim traders forced close to 10 million sub-Saharan Africans into slavery well before the Portuguese expeditions of the 1400s. Merchants from Muslim cities and kingdoms in North Africa and the Middle East operated this network, which leading academics believe lasted from the seventh to eighteenth centuries. One of the main reasons this slave network developed and prospered was that Islamic law prohibited the enslavement of Muslims by other Muslims. Some of the captured Africans worked in homes and fields owned by well-to-do Muslims. These included sugar plantations in Egypt and Syria and other parts of the Middle East. Other black slaves were persuaded to convert to Islam and achieved the status of soldiers in Muslim armies.

As time went on, Europeans recognized the economic potential of the Muslim plantation and became drawn to the social and economic structure it created. Some of the first Europeans to adopt this model were merchants and wealthy landowners in Genoa, a kingdom in northern Italy. The Genoese imitated the Muslims by establishing sugar plantations on the eastern Mediterranean island of Cyprus and acquiring Africans to labor on these plantations. To obtain these workers, the Genoese tapped into the trans-Saharan slave network.

Genoese plantations became extremely profitable. Not surprisingly, one of Genoa's main European trade rivals, Portugal, eventually established its own sugar plantations. In the 1440s and 1450s, Portuguese plantations cropped up on the Cape Verde, Madeira, and Canary islands, all situated off of Africa's northwestern coast. At first, these operations utilized cheap European laborers, including condemned prisoners. But as it became increasingly difficult to fill the demand for workers, plantation owners turned to importing African slaves.

The Atlantic Trade Develops

For years the Portuguese controlled most of the Atlantic slave trade, which at first was confined to the ocean's eastern sector, near Portugal and Africa. But other Europeans began to see that such cheap labor could be useful in their newly founded colonies in the Americas. Spain led the way in this enterprise—it was rapidly building an overseas empire of colonies throughout the Caribbean and Central and South America. Initially, the Spanish bought most of their African slaves from Portuguese slave traders, but beginning in the 1640s Spain and Portugal became bitter enemies when Portugal revolted and the dual monarchy between the two nations ended. Thereafter the Spanish got the bulk of their slaves from the Dutch, French, and English, who had already begun to expand their slaving activities to supply their own overseas colonies.

England's involvement in the Atlantic trade demonstrates the success that these nations enjoyed from exploiting Africa for slaves. Between 1627 and 1643, the English brought some 6,000 Africans to work on plantations at their colony on the

An illustration depicting Arab traders bringing captured African villagers
to the east coast of Africa as part of the slave trade

African Slaves in Hispaniola

The case of the large Caribbean island of Hispaniola is a typical example of how the practice of slavery developed over time. By 1515, Spanish plantation owners on the island had worked to death or murdered about 200,000 of the island's original 250,000 inhabitants. And by the mid-1600s, all of the original inhabitants had been exterminated. To replace them, the colonists first tried shipping in cheap white European laborers, including convicts and orphans. However, as large supplies of the latter became scarce, this approach proved too expensive. Hispaniola's wealthy white elite responded by importing Africans, at first purchased from Portuguese traders but later supplied by the French, Dutch, and English.

Caribbean island of Barbados. And by 1667, more than 40,000 Africans lived and worked on Barbados—nearly twice the number of white colonists on the island.

Along with the English, the Dutch, French, Portuguese, and other Europeans managed to reap huge profits from what became known as the "triangular trade." This commercial slave network featured three main legs, forming a giant triangle that spanned the Atlantic. The first leg consisted of the export of goods from Europe to Africa, where African leaders exchanged people for commodities such as gunpowder, fine fabrics, and liquor. The second leg of the triangle entailed the sale of the slaves in the American colonies. And the third and final leg was the sale of products made by the colonial slaves—among them spices, cotton, tobacco, sugar, and molasses—to Europe.

The Trade's Impact in Africa

The effects of the ongoing Atlantic slave trade in western Africa were far-reaching. First, the vast majority of the peoples in the region either participated in the trade or were victimized by it. Historians have identified at least 173 African tribes, kingdoms, city-states, or other local groups that participated in one way or another over the centuries. Among the larger, more powerful western African states that took part were the Songhai and Bamana kingdoms (in present-day Mali); the Saalum, Jolof, and Denanke nations (in what is now Senegal); the Kuba and Luba empires (in present-day Congo); and the Ndongo kingdom (in today's Angola).

One thing that these and the other peoples of western Africa had in common was that they, like the Europeans and Muslims, accepted the idea of slavery. It had existed in the region well before outsiders penetrated sub-Saharan Africa, and in those times it was common for one African state to capture and enslave members of neighboring states. When the Muslims and Europeans arrived looking for slaves, it seemed only natural for some local leaders to seek profits by supplying them with slaves.

It should be pointed out, however, that African slave owners tended to treat their slaves more benevolently than the Europeans did. And at first African leaders and merchants did not realize that the people they sold to these outsiders would in many cases be treated brutally. Rather, they expected that the slaves would become laborers who, though unfree, would be treated humanely.

Over time, the corruption and inhumanity of the trade became widely known. Nevertheless only a small contingent of Africans refused to go on supplying the white traders; most others continued doing so. As Chancellor Williams explains, "Many Africans became enmeshed in the horrors of the trade, knew what they were doing and, in the pursuit of . . . riches, became as brutal as the whites in dealing with their own kind."

African Slavery Less Harsh

Although the peoples of West Africa practiced slavery, there were some important differences between African slavery and European slavery. African slaves were comparable in a number of ways to European indentured servants. They were given small wages for their work and under certain conditions were allowed to gain their freedom. Also, African slaves sometimes became respected artisans and trusted members of their masters' families and communities. In addition, in many African states it was illegal for a master to work a slave to the point of exhaustion or to draw blood while punishing a slave.

Those Africans who participated in the trade were also lured by commodities other than money. Guns were particularly desirable. "Black leaders saw these new weapons of death as the source of the white man's power and the immediate threat to their own existence," Williams writes. And "the Africans became insistent in their demands for guns as articles of trade." Accordingly, those African states that gained large supplies of guns could "then seek to become big, wealthy powers, expanding their territories over weaker black states, and capturing millions of prisoners to be enslaved in the process."

As a result, wars among neighboring Africans motivated by the desire to capture slaves became common and often devastating for all involved. These conflicts not only ravaged entire communities and caused some kingdoms to decline, but also played right into the hands of the European powers that wanted to further weaken Africa and its peoples. According to Williams, some European leaders saw that their supplying guns "would be a built-in motivation for perpetual warfare among the blacks themselves, creating an everlasting hatred

An engraving (circa 1858) of slaves in the British West Indies
working in sugar cane fields on a plantation

between groups, destroying every basis for unity, and, above all, firearms would keep them so busily hating and fighting each other that they would forget their real enemies, the [white Europeans]."

In fact, large parts of Africa were so damaged by the slave trade that they remained weak and vulnerable even after the Europeans banned the trade. And that made them easy prey for the next major phase of European exploitation, which would turn out to be even more destructive and demoralizing than the last one.

Chapter Five:
A New Round of European Explorers

Although most Europeans had long lacked any moral qualms about perpetuating the African slave trade, there had always been a few who objected. And as time went on, that segment of Europe's population grew larger. Racked by guilt, they formed an abolitionist movement that rapidly gained momentum in the second half of the eighteenth century. Demands to end the African slave trade first took root in England and France, and then spread over Europe and eventually across the Atlantic to the newly formed United States. The British abolished the trade in 1807, and U.S. legislators followed their lead the next year. Britain banned slavery itself in 1834 and by the end of that decade most other nations had done the same. Slavery persisted in the United States until 1865, following the close of the Civil War.

Abolitionists hoped to compensate for the cruelties that the slave trade had long heaped on Africa. They proposed to do this by converting as many Africans as possible to Christianity. They also sought to revitalize local African economies by modernizing agriculture and expanding trade in goods other than slaves. As Robert July explains, the reformers naïvely believed that "slavery would shrivel and die . . . while Western, Christian culture would gradually take hold, leading the Africans from what was regarded as a primitive barbarism to the higher civilizations of the West." To this end, they began organizing numerous groups of missionaries, traders, and aid workers to be sent into the African interior.

But that immense region was still largely uncharted, and before any serious restoration or modernization of Africa could take place, its territory had to be explored thoroughly. July continues:

> At first European enterprise took the form of a series of expeditions to investigate the interior, and particularly to determine the course of the Niger [River], as a means of opening up the country to legitimate trade from Europe. Such was the motivation which lay behind the major explorers of the early nineteenth century.

The grandiose, well-meaning goals of these individuals were concisely summed up by one of the most famous of their number, Scottish missionary David Livingstone. His motto was "Christianity, Commerce, and Civilization."

To the Niger and Great Lakes

One of the first Europeans to devote most of his career to bringing Africa's little-known regions to the world's attention was Scottish physician and explorer Mungo Park. In 1794, at the request of the British government, he set out to plot the course of the Niger River. A leading British official told him, "The great object of your journey will be to pursue the course of this river to the utmost possible distance to which it can be traced; to establish communication . . . with the different nations on the banks; [and] to obtain all the local knowledge in your power [about] them."

Following this directive, Park traveled along the Niger from 1796 to 1797, collected large amounts of information about the region and its peoples, and then went back to Britain to great acclaim. He returned to Africa in 1804, hoping to prove that the Niger and Congo were one and the same river (which is not the case). During this quest, however, he encountered hostile locals who attacked and killed him in 1806 along the Niger.

Park was among the early nineteenth-century explorers and missionaries who inspired one of the greatest European explorers of that era: Sir Richard Francis Burton of England. Burton was a soldier, scholar, and linguist who spoke twenty-nine European, African, and Asian languages. In the 1850s he began exploring the so-called Great Lakes region of east-central Africa, striving to learn about the peoples of the area and to locate the source of the Nile River.

An illustration of Simon's Bay, in South Africa, from Scottish explorer Mungo Park's 1797 book *Travels in the Interior Districts of Africa*

In February 1858 Burton reached Lake Tanganyika, which, with an area of 12,700 square miles (33,020 square kilometers), is one of the largest freshwater lakes in the world. On the return trek, he fell ill. While he was recovering, his associate, British soldier and explorer John Hanning Speke, traveled northward and came upon Lake Victoria. Speke was the first European to see that majestic waterway. In addition to being Africa's largest lake, it is one of the main sources of the Nile (although at the time this was not completely clear). In the years that followed, Burton and Speke became rivals and enemies—Speke was a supporter of imperialistic policies and thought that Europeans should exploit Africa, whereas Burton truly wanted to help the Africans.

Explorer of the Century

Another avid adventurer of that era was David Livingstone. He arrived in Africa in 1840 at the age of twenty-seven, eager to serve as a missionary and physician. He went on to spend most of the rest of his life in Africa and became the most renowned explorer of that century. His influence was immense; he "fired the imagination and ambition of many other explorers, whether missionaries or not," comments British scholar of African history Basil Davidson.

One reason that Livingstone was so successful was that he put the Africans he met at ease and earned their trust. He traveled very lightly and, instead of soldiers armed to the teeth, took with him only a few porters and other helpers. Also, as a missionary he did not force Christian ideas on people or condemn their existing beliefs. Rather, he preached only to those who expressed interest and encouraged his converts to teach others. As a result he was usually well received and made many friends.

A highlight of Livingstone's career occurred in 1855. While exploring along the Zambezi River, in southeastern Africa, he became the first European to see one of the biggest and most beautiful waterfalls on the continent. The local people referred to it as Mosi-oa-Tunya, meaning "the smoke that thunders;" he called it Victoria Falls after Britain's reigning queen, Victoria.

In 1866, Livingstone moved northward toward the Great Lakes region in hopes of finding the source of the Nile. Burton and Speke had suggested only a few years before that Lake Victoria might be the source (which was partially accurate); but Livingstone disagreed—he thought the major source was more likely located farther south. And after stumbling on the Lualaba River, he mistakenly identified it as a section of the Nile.

Like Many Small Comets

Livingstone later colorfully described his approach to the splendid Victoria Falls, saying:

[At first] one sees nothing but a dense white cloud, which, at the time . . . had two bright rainbows on it. From this cloud rushed up a great jet of vapor exactly like steam, and it mounted 200 or 300 feet high; there condensing, it changed its hue to that of dark smoke, and came back in a constant shower, which soon wetted us to the skin. [One of] the columns of vapor . . . leaps quite clear of the rock, and [then it breaks into] pieces of water, all rushing on in the same direction. . . . The snow-white sheet[s of water] seemed like myriads of small comets rushing on in one direction, each of which left behind its nucleus rays of foam.

An illustration of the historic meeting between Welsh explorer and journalist Henry Morton Stanley and Scottish missionary Dr. David Livingstone in Ujiji, Tanzania, on the shores of Lake Tanganyika on November 10, 1871

Stanley Meets Livingstone

During his extensive travels, Livingstone contracted a number of serious illnesses, including cholera, and eventually fell out of touch with the outside world for several years. As time went on, rumors about the widely popular national hero spread across Europe and even to North America. Some claimed he was dead; others suggested that some savage tribe was holding him captive; and newspapers constantly posed the question of his whereabouts. In 1871, George Bennett, publisher of the *New York Herald*, hired the noted Welsh-American journalist Henry Morton Stanley to locate Livingstone. When Stanley asked how much he could spend on the expedition, Bennett gave him the now famous answer:

> Draw a thousand pounds now; and when you have gone through that, draw another thousand, and when that is spent, draw another thousand, and when you have finished that, draw another thousand, and so on; but, find Livingstone!

Stanley reached eastern Africa in March 1871 and at the head of some two hundred men immediately marched inland. After following a series of leads, eight months later he found Livingstone in a tiny village near Lake Tanganyika. Modern scholars differ about Stanley's now well-known query, "Dr. Livingstone, I presume?" Some think he did say it, as he claimed he did. Others feel it may have been fabricated later to dramatize the legendary initial meeting between the two men.

Many More Surprises

Stanley went on to bring important knowledge of the peoples of the central African interior to the outside world. As had been the case with the Portuguese and other Europeans in centuries

A White Man With a Gray Beard

Stanley later recalled his legendary first meeting with Livingstone this way:

I pushed back the crowds, and, passing from the rear, walked down a living avenue of people until I came in front of the semicircle of [locals], in the front of which stood [a] white man with the gray beard. As I advanced slowly toward him I . . . did not know how he would receive me; so I did what cowardice and false pride suggested was the best thing—walked deliberately to him, took off my hat, and said, "Dr. Livingstone, I presume?" "Yes," said he, with a kind smile, lifting his cap slightly.

Henry Morton Stanley

MR. H. M. STANLEY,
Photographed at Sandringham, April 28th, 1890, on his return from the Emin Pasha Expedition.

F. RALPH,   (COPYRIGHT.)   DERSINGHAM.

past, he was genuinely surprised at how civilized and sophisticated many African leaders and their subjects were.

In 1874, during another expedition financed jointly by the *New York Herald* and the *Daily Telegraph* of Britain, he aimed to trace the course of the Congo River from the interior to the Atlantic Ocean. Along the way, he observed numerous local kingdoms and cultures.

One of these, the Ugandan kingdom of the Ganda people, struck Stanley as especially impressive. Its king, Mutesa, was not a brutal savage, as third-hand reports filtering back to Europe had claimed. Rather, the explorer wrote, Mutesa was "a pious Muslim and an intelligent, humane king [who was] loved more than hated, respected more than feared." Moreover, the kingdom was well ordered, had a sound legal system, and enjoyed considerable prosperity.

Other surprising, impressive, and/or fascinating revelations about Africa came from several other Europeans who visited the continent. French-American anthropologist Paul du Chaillu set out to see if some ancient Greek legends were true. These accounts claimed that a race of Pygmies, or very small people, dwelled somewhere in the African interior. In 1865 he managed to locate a tribe of Pygmies along the Ogowe River, in west-central Africa. (Other Pygmy groups were later found elsewhere, both inside and outside of Africa.) Du Chaillu recalled his first encounter with a Pygmy, whom, out of ignorance, he called a dwarf:

> "A dwarf!" I shouted, as the little creature came out [of her hut]. "A woman!" I shouted again. "A pygmy!" The little creature shrieked [and] her piercing wail rent the air. What a sight! I had never seen the like before. . . . How frightened she was! She trembled all over. She was neither white nor black; she was of a yellow, or mulatto color. . . . I cannot tell you how delighted I was.

Du Chaillu was also the first European to see and describe gorillas, who up to that time had been no less legendary than the Pygmies.

Thanks to these and other explorations by nineteenth-century Europeans, large sections of Africa became known to the outside world for the first time. In some ways this was good, but for many Africans, unfortunately, the bad initially outweighed the good. Although explorers like Livingstone and Stanley were well meaning, their efforts unveiled to the major European powers Africa's enormous material and human resources. And in the eyes of these leaders, Africa was ripe for exploitation. One of history's largest and most devastating episodes of imperialism, colonialism, and greed was about to begin.

Chapter Six:
Europe's Mad Scramble for Africa

In 1857, David Livingstone pleaded with his fellow Europeans about Africa, saying: "I beg to direct your attention to Africa. . . . Do not let it be shut again! I go back to Africa to try to make an open path for commerce and Christianity. [Please] carry out the work which I have begun. I leave it with you!"

In the decades that followed, most Europeans did "direct their attention to Africa," but not in the way that Livingstone had intended. In public, European leaders claimed to want only the best for Africa. Typical was the goal stated by Belgium's King Leopold II: "To open to civilization the only part of our globe where it has yet to penetrate, to pierce the darkness which envelops whole populations, it is, I dare say, a crusade worthy of this century of progress."

Behind the scenes, however, European attitudes and words were less noble and far more selfish. For example, Leopold revealed his actual plans for a Belgian colony in Africa in a brief but devastating statement made in private to a Belgian official: "I do not want to risk . . . losing a fine chance to secure for ourselves a slice of this magnificent African cake."

The motives for what became known as the "scramble for Africa," in which Europeans began slicing up that cake, were political, economic, and cultural. From a political standpoint, the great powers wanted to seize and colonize various regions of Africa in order either to create overseas empires or expand the ones they already had.

Economically speaking, Africa had been shown to possess abundant raw materials, including cotton, coal, rubber, copper, tin, gold, and other precious metals. Having African colonies would enable Europe to extract huge amounts of these commodities. Moreover, this undertaking could be carried out utilizing cheap labor, since African workers could be paid far less than European ones.

The chief cultural reason for exploiting Africa stemmed from the rampant racism that pervaded white European society. Most whites viewed themselves as unquestionably superior to African blacks, who were considered primitive, backward, and even savage. The prevailing common wisdom was that, in colonizing and exploiting the Africans, Europeans would be doing them a major favor.

The Berlin Conference

It was Belgium's King Leopold who carried the torch for Europe into Africa. In the 1870s, his envoys approached African leaders in the vast Congo region and persuaded them to sign various treaties. These documents were usually fraudulent—one European eyewitness pointed out that they were often several pages long, written in a language that the Congolese could not understand, and purposely designed to mislead. Leaders typically signed an "X" at the bottom, unaware that they were being hoodwinked. By signing, local chiefs in the Congo unwittingly allowed Leopold to gain control of much of the region. Not long afterward, other major powers, among them France, Germany, Britain, and the United States, recognized his claims. Their recognition gave de facto

A drawing of Leopold I, the first king of Belgium and
Queen Victoria's uncle, in a ceremonial uniform

legal status to the corporate, privately owned entity he was
creating—the so-called Congo Free State. (At first, Leopold's
venture in Africa was not formally sponsored or officially con-
doned by the Belgian government.)

With this green light, Leopold began assembling forces
to capitalize on his new African holdings. He was careful, of
course, to cloak his real intentions in earnest-sounding claims
of humanitarian aims. This veil of good intentions gained him
political favor in the form of a helpful public endorsement. In
October 1884 London's *Daily Telegraph* proclaimed that the
Belgian king had "knit adventurers, traders, and missionaries
of many races into one band of men . . . to carry into the inte-

rior of Africa new ideas of law, order, humanity, and protection of the natives."

Other European leaders were perfectly aware of what Leopold was actually doing, for they had similar aims. They also realized that a large-scale international competition was on the horizon, with the outcome very possibly being military conflicts among these nations. Hoping to avoid major confrontations and hostilities, the great powers decided to hold a meeting. The object of this summit was to draw up mutually agreeable rules for partitioning, or dividing up, the African continent.

The gathering took place from November 1884 through February 1885 in Berlin, Germany, and became known as the Berlin Conference. In attendance were delegates from Britain, France, Germany, Austria-Hungary, Russia, Portugal, Denmark, Spain, Italy, the Netherlands, Sweden, Belgium, Turkey, and the United States. They drew up an agreement

Promises Not Kept

In Article 6 of the Berlin Act, the nations involved vowed to do what was best for the Africans, a promise few Europeans actually kept:

All the powers exercising sovereign rights or influence in the aforesaid territories bind themselves to watch over the preservation of the native tribes, and to care for the improvement of the conditions of their moral and material well-being. . . . They shall, without distinction of creed or nation, protect and favor all religious, scientific, or charitable institutions and undertakings created and organized for the above ends, or which aim at instructing the natives and bringing home to them the blessings of civilization.

known as the Berlin Act of 1885. The pact stated that any one of these powers could claim ownership of essentially any African state or region it wanted, as long as it could obtain and then maintain physical control of that entity. The occupying nation was required to notify the other great powers that it was taking possession of an entity, in case the other nations wanted to dispute the affair. Another major provision of the Berlin Act held that all of its signers would be allowed free trade and shipping rights throughout most of Africa.

A Place in the Sun

Looking in retrospect at the agreement signed in Berlin, it is stunning by today's standards to consider that the nations of Africa were not represented at all—they contributed neither at the conference nor to the actual signing of the agreement. The city-states, tribes, and kingdoms of Africa had no say in the impending division and colonization of their own continent.

As soon as the treaty entered effect, agents of the European powers poured into Africa and, as Leopold's operatives had done before, tricked the indigenous peoples into signing over their lands. Some of the so-called treaties were signed because the agents brought heavily armed soldiers with them and blatantly employed the threat of violence. Soon, comments distinguished British author Thomas Pakenham, the "gun—not trade or the cross—became the symbol of the age in Africa." In fact, he adds, Europe "imposed its will on Africa at the point of a gun."

Through swift action and forceful tactics, European nations managed to partition Africa extremely quickly. In 1875, a mere handful of European colonies existed there; but by 1914, a very large proportion of the continent had been colonized by or otherwise brought under the control of the European powers. At that point, Britain, France, Germany, and Belgium alone held and exploited roughly 61 percent of Africa's territory.

A 1916 illustration from France's *L'Illustration* of hand-to-hand combat between German and South African troops in Bois d'Elville, nicknamed Devil's Wood, near Longueval, France

Germany was among the first of the great powers to acquire pieces of Africa. In the mid-1880s it declared as protectorates (territories under its control) Togoland (on the Guinea coast), the Cameroons (lying north of the Congo), and South-West Africa (now Nambia). A few years later, German leader Kaiser Wilhelm II said in a public speech:

> We have conquered for ourselves a place in the sun. It will now be my task to see to it that this place in the sun shall remain our undisputed possession, in order that the sun's rays may fall fruitfully upon our activity and trade in foreign parts, that our industry and agriculture may develop within the state and our sailing sports upon the water. . . . As head of the Empire I therefore rejoice over every citizen . . . who goes forth with this large outlook and seeks new points where we can drive in the nail on which to hang our armor.

In similar fashion, France, which already controlled Algeria (in northern Africa), now occupied nearby Tunisia and large areas in western Africa (including modern Senegal, Mali, and Benin). Britain entered Egypt (which held strong influence over the adjoining Sudan) and took control of what are now Nigeria, Kenya, Uganda, and South Africa. Also, Italy gained sway over Eritrea (north of Ethiopia), Somaliland (east of Ethiopia), and Cyrenaica (now Libya).

Catastrophe in the Congo

All of these countries ruled their African colonies and territories to one degree or another with what might be called strong-arm tactics. The indigenous peoples were not free and were obliged to follow the rules made by the local colonial power. Tens of millions of people were not allowed to decide their own destinies. Some were pushed off of their ancestral lands by white farmers and in some cases, if they tried to resist, jailed or even killed.

Nowhere was European conquest, occupation, and exploitation more brutal and tragic than in Leopold's Congo. Essentially his own private domain, the colony was seventy-six times larger than Belgium and covered an enormous 7 percent of the African continent. The state's official name, the Congo Free State, was highly deceptive. Its 30 million residents were not only unfree, but treated almost literally like slaves. Many of them were forced to do backbreaking, dangerous labor on farms that grew a large, spongy vine from which a valuable kind of liquid latex rubber was harvested. The bodies of these unfortunate workers became coated with the liquid as they worked. And at the end of the workday they had to peel the hardened rubber off, which was extremely painful.

This was only the proverbial tip of the iceberg of Leopold's abuses. To ensure that the laborers continued working without complaint, he unleashed on them an army of henchmen, who routinely beat, raped, mutilated, and murdered them for the slightest infraction. Sometimes Leopold's strongmen committed these atrocities simply to keep the Congolese in a constant state of fear. Modern estimates for the death toll in the Congo vary; they range from as low as 5 million to as high as 20 million, with the causes being murder, starvation, and disease—in the twenty years of Leopold's reign.

Eventually, outsiders, including several Western journalists, found out what was happening in the Congo. They collected evidence of Leopold's criminal acts and alerted the world. Many of the countries that had once supported his seizure of the country then condemned him and called for an end to the abuses. Accordingly, in 1908 the Belgian government took away his African holdings and began administering them more humanely under a new name, the Belgian Congo. Many people today find it shocking that Leopold was never punished for his misdeeds. He did lose his private empire and become hated by many of his subjects (who would boo him during

Leopold Accused of Crimes

American politician and historian George W. Williams was one of many outspoken critics who denounced Leopold and his abuses in the Congo. After investigating conditions in the Congo first hand, he issued an open letter to the Belgian king, saying in part:

> [I accuse you of] deceit, fraud, robberies, arson, murder, slave-raiding, and general policy of cruelty. . . . All the crimes perpetrated in the Congo have been done in your name, and you must answer at the bar of Public Sentiment for the misgovernment of a people, whose lives and fortunes were entrusted to you. . . . I now appeal to the [Great] Powers [to] call and create an International Commission to investigate [abuses in the Congo and] I appeal to the Belgian people and to their Constitutional Government . . . to cleanse itself from the [charge] of the crimes with which your Majesty's personal State of Congo is polluted.

PUNCH, OR THE LONDON CHARIVARI.—NOVEMBER 28, 1906.

IN THE RUBBER COILS.

Scene—The Congo "Free" State.

A 1906 cartoon depicting King Leopold II, king of the Belgians, crushing the Congo with rubber coils

his funeral). Yet until he died in 1909, he remained king and retained his vast personal fortune.

News of Leopold's abuses incited better treatment of the Congolese people; but it did not end European colonialism in Africa. The great powers still ruled large sectors of the continent—and no nation controlled more of it than Britain. The British increasingly encountered local resistance; however, neither they nor any other Europeans yet foresaw that the days of their interference in Africa were numbered.

Chapter Seven:
British Imperialism in Africa

Although Britain was not the only European nation that intervened in Africa both before and during the scramble of the 1800s, its presence there was unique because its holdings in Africa were part of something much larger. In the 1700s and especially in the 1800s, the British built a worldwide empire that dwarfed those of its European rivals. Britain came to control territories on practically every continent, inspiring the famous phrase, "the sun never sets on the British Empire." And the lands over which Britain held sway in Africa were nothing short of enormous. By 1914, it controlled fully 30 percent of the continent. That was far more than any other outside power.

It is important to note that few of Britain's foreign holdings, including those in Africa, were official colonies. Instead, most often the British used their massive global navy and considerable economic and political influence to meddle in and often control foreign markets. In doing so, they forced nations and entire regions to become heavily financially dependent on trade with Britain. And in that way these peoples and regions became part of its growing empire. To maintain its relationships with those peoples, Britain sometimes negotiated treaties. But just as often it used its considerable military might to impose and enforce its will. In Africa, Britain liberally employed both of these tools—treaties (always weighted in favor of Britain) and armed force.

The White Man's Burden

Today, many people look back at the nineteenth century and find it disturbing that Britain and other nations brazenly seized control of lands and peoples in Africa and elsewhere. By modern standards, such imperialist policies seem arrogant, unfair, and destructive. But at the time, most Europeans saw things very differently. Most British leaders, thinkers, and traders, for instance, believed that the foreigners under their rule ultimately benefited from imperialist policies. They argued that Britain was providing roads, ports, housing, industry, and jobs in poor, underdeveloped lands. Additionally, they introduced education, law and order, and Christianity, advancements that helped to civilize the "backward natives."

In fact, many British took this line of reasoning a step further and considered it their actual duty to do these things. As members of a "superior" white culture, they claimed, it was only right that they teach the arts of civilization to those non-whites who lacked them. This so-called responsibility came to be called the "white man's burden."

British leaders felt they had a particularly large burden to bear in Africa; they viewed black Africans as more savage and inferior than other peoples they had encountered abroad. Therefore, though they sought to civilize the Africans, they believed that it was not realistic to trust or befriend them—at least at first. British writer R. M. Ballantyne summed up this attitude in 1879:

Helping the "Silent, Sullen Peoples"

The term "white man's burden" came from the title of a famous poem penned by British writer Rudyard Kipling in 1865. It reads in part:

> Take up the White Man's burden—
> No tawdry rule of kings,
> But toil of serf and sweeper—
> The tale of common things.
> The ports ye shall not enter,
> The roads ye shall not tread,
> Go mark them with your living,
> And mark them with your dead. . . .
> Take up the White Man's burden—
> Ye dare not stoop to less—
> Nor call too loud on Freedom
> To cloak your weariness;
> By all ye cry or whisper,
> By all ye leave or do,
> The silent, sullen peoples
> Shall weigh your gods and you.

A cartoon portraying English poet Rudyard Kipling writing in the Indian bush and watched by a snake and a lion

To treat [the native African] kindly, justly, considerately, lovingly; to try to do him every possible good, and chiefly, to bring his soul in contact with the Savior [Jesus Christ], is our simple duty, but to trust him is no part of our duty. It is worse than folly because it defeats our philanthropic [charitable] views and prolongs his debasement. Who would trust a thief, a liar, or a murderer? The whole [African] nation, root and branch, is a huge thief [and] an inveterate [chronic] liar.

A British military officer in eastern Africa, F. D. Lugard, shared Ballantyne's view that Africans were inferior to white Europeans. In 1893, when British imperialism in Africa was nearing its height, he stated:

The essential point in dealing with Africans is to establish a respect for the European. Upon this—the prestige of the white man—depends his influence, often his very existence, in Africa. If he shows by his surroundings, by his assumption of superiority, that he is far above the native, he will be respected. . . . It is the greatest possible mistake to suppose that a European can acquire a greater influence by adopting the mode of life of the natives. In effect, it is to lower himself to their plane, instead of elevating them to his.

The British in Egypt

The first large African territory that Britain came to dominate was Egypt. In 1798, France's strong military general Napoleon Bonaparte invaded Egypt, a move that alarmed the British because much of their valuable commerce with faraway India passed through Egypt. The British responded by dispatching a fleet that promptly crushed the French fleet lying

A hand-colored engraving of a nineteenth-century painting by
Jean-Leon Gerome of Napoleon and the Sphinx during
the French invasion of Egypt in 1798

off of the Egyptian Mediterranean coast. After that defeat
Napoleon abandoned his land troops in Egypt and British soldiers entered the country and defeated the remaining derelict
French troops. For a while the British thought that they had
acquired a permanent protectorate in Africa. But in 1807 a
tenacious Egyptian leader, Mohammed Ali, delivered them a
decisive defeat and they withdrew.

Britain's attention returned to Egypt in the 1860s, when the
French and Egyptians jointly constructed the Suez Canal, the
waterway that linked the Mediterranean with the Red Sea and
Indian Ocean. Again worried about their route to India, the
British sought an excuse to intervene in Egypt. Their chance
came in 1882. A local rebellion threatened to undermine the
nearly bankrupt Egyptian government, so Britain sent in
troops—supposedly to stabilize the country. A British official and viceroy of Egypt, the Earl of Cromer, illuminated the
official reason for British intervention:

Egypt may now almost be said to form part of Europe. It is on the high road to the Far East [and especially India]. The special aptitude shown by Englishmen in the government of [eastern] races pointed to England as the most effective and beneficent instrument for the gradual introduction of European civilization into Egypt. An Anglo-French, or an Anglo-Italian occupation . . . would have been detrimental to Egyptian interests.

Whether or not the British takeover of Egypt best served the interests of Egypt is questionable. Some historians consider Britain's interest in Egypt at the time to be a prime example of political imperialism, or a policy essentially pursued to ensure that Britain maintained its leverage in the international order and that the balance of power did not tip.

The takeover of Egypt also gave Britain convenient access to the Sudan, an enormous territory lying largely to the southwest. The French also had their sights set on the Sudan, and in 1898 a small French army occupied the Sudanese town of Fushoda. British soldiers hurried to the scene and after a tense standoff the French backed down and departed, allowing the Sudan to fall under British control.

The British v. the Zulus

One of the reasons that the British wanted to occupy the Sudan was because of its geographical position in Africa. By that time, Britain had taken control of numerous other African lands, including Nigeria and Kenya in central Africa and much of what is present-day South Africa. The leading British imperialists dreamed of creating an unbroken chain of possessions from Egypt southward to Cape Town, South Africa.

A Zulu hut in the South African province of KwaZulu-Natal

They came to call it a "Cape to Cairo" empire, and the Sudan was a key link in that proposed chain.

The manner in which Britain gained power over South Africa vividly shows how their African empire began to take shape. In the 1700s, rounding the Cape of Good Hope was an important route for European traders heading for the Far East. In 1795 it appeared that France might seize the Cape region, so the British grabbed it first. They returned Cape Town to the Dutch in 1803, only to take it back three years later.

As time went on, Britain encountered increasing resistance to its rule in South Africa, partly from local leaders. The more the colony expanded into the interior, the more it intruded into the lands of indigenous peoples.

A Marvelous Escape

A young British officer named Horace Smith-Dorrien later recalled how he managed to survive the slaughter at Isandlwana:

Before we knew [what was happening], they [the Zulus] came right into the camp, [stabbing] everyone right and left. Everybody then who had a horse turned to fly. [I] had lots of marvelous escapes, and was firing away at them with my revolver as I galloped along. The ground there down to the river was so broken that the Zulus went as fast as the horses and kept killing all the way. [I escaped by plunging] into the river, [where] a loose horse came by and I got hold of his tail and he landed me safely on the other bank.

The fiercest resistance of all came from the Zulus, who built a small but powerful state in southeastern Africa in the early-to-mid 1800s. Border disputes between the Zulus and whites came to a head in the 1870s. And in 1879 local British officials issued an ultimatum to the Zulu king, Cetshwayo, warning him to give in to British demands. When the king ignored the ultimatum, British forces invaded Zululand.

At first, Cetshwayo and his large, well-trained army acquitted themselves well. They handed the British one of their worst defeats ever at a place called Isandlwana, a battle in which nearly half of the British contingent was wiped out. Despite this important Zulu victory, the British, with their seemingly endless supply of troops and advanced weapons, went on to win the war. The Zulus lost their independence and were incorporated into Britain's widening sphere of influence.

The British v. the Boers

The Zulus were not the only objectors to Britain's presence in South Africa. To the irritation of the British, much of the opposition they encountered there over the years came from white settlers. By the time Britain took long-term charge of the Cape, the Boers were well entrenched in the colony's inland areas. These conservative Christians strongly objected when Britain banned slavery in the colony (and in all of its other possessions) in 1834. In their view, slavery was ordained by God. As Thomas Pakenham explains:

> In their conflicts with black people, [the Boers] were uniquely uncompromising. . . . The Boers on the frontier conceded no equality to [black] Africans in Church or state. And the land seemed to be theirs for the taking, the land belonging to Africans who were still poorer, weaker, and less united than the Boers. To work this land,

A hand-colored engraving depicting the Boers attacking a British armored train during the Second Boer War, 1899-1902

like the settlers of the American South and the Caribbean, the Boers took Africans as slaves.

Citing British slavery policy and other grievances, most of the Boers packed up their belongings and abandoned their farms. Between 1835 and 1837 they migrated farther inland, beyond the colony's boundaries. Following this so-called Great Trek, they established two independent Boer states: the Transvaal and the Orange Free State.

However, this was not enough to escape the ever-reaching grasp of British imperialism. Britain eventually decided that it was in its best interest to incorporate the Boer nations into its growing African empire. In 1877 the British boldly seized the Transvaal. After a series of protests and negotiations, however, they conceded the country self-rule—as long as it recognized Britain as its overriding protector. But then the Boers rose in revolt. They were so successful in what became known as the First Boer War (1880-1881) that the British withdrew.

Many more troubles between the British and Boers ensued, climaxing in the Second Boer War (1899-1902). Britain won, and the Boers very reluctantly accepted British rule. But this proved a hollow victory, for a momentous new era was about to dawn. Whether ruled by Britain, or France, or some other outside power, all African peoples yearned for freedom and self-rule.

Chapter Eight:
Africans Throw off the European Yoke

In retrospect, people today readily see a remarkable reality that the Europeans of prior centuries did not—namely that Europe's long-term exploitation and domination of Africa ultimately was doomed to fail by its very nature. By forcing themselves on the Africans, European nations could not help but allow Africa to learn more about how they and the outside world operated. And that allowed the Africans to adapt in ways that made them stronger, more resilient, and more self-sufficient. As Robert July ably put it,

> [European colonialism in Africa] contained the germ of its own destruction; indeed, the whole colonial system was a vast engine for the creation of a modern self-governing Africa. By conquering, colonialism caused the desire to be free. By exploiting, it produced a rising resistance to tyranny. By introducing Africa to the modern world, it generated visions of a better life consummated in liberty. By demonstrating

its own fallibility, it begot the hope that led to autonomy [independence].

Forces for Independence

For these reasons strong nationalist feelings swept throughout the African continent in the twentieth century. (Nationalism is the desire for and promotion of the independence and self-rule of a separate people or cultural group.) At first, such feelings and ideas took hold among a handful of educated African intellectuals, thinkers, and farsighted political figures. But during and after World War I these ideas began to disseminate and influence popular thought. As that devastating conflict pitted the great European powers against one another, it showed Africans that these nations were not invincible. Moreover, the war's principal loser, Germany, had to give up its African colonies, demonstrating how colonies could be swept away by major political and military events.

Inspired by such realities, fifty-seven African and pro-African delegates from fifteen countries met in Paris in 1919 in the first of several Pan-African Congresses. They called for fair treatment of Africans, including improved education throughout Africa. They also stated: "The natives of Africa must have the right to participate in the government . . . in conformity with the principle that the government exists for the natives, and not the natives for the government." This and other pan-African meetings that followed in the 1920s made news around the world. As a result, scholar Basil Davidson writes, "little by little, and then with gathering speed, the nationalist cause spread far outside the limits of [Africa's] educated minority . . . and assumed mass dimensions as it drew within its orbit ever larger numbers of townspeople and peasants."

One important facet of these nationalist sentiments was the realization by African leaders that the solution to their problems lay not in seeking revenge for what Europeans had done in the past. Rather, success as independent nations would come

A poster titled "Day of the African Army and Colonial Troops" by
Lucien Hector Jonas during the first World War, 1914-1918

when Africans took responsibility for themselves and learned to solve their own problems. This progressive attitude was well summarized by the widely respected Ghanaian leader Kwame Nkrumah:

> For centuries, Europeans dominated the African continent. The white man [claimed to want] to "civilize" Africa. Under this cloak, the Europeans robbed the continent of vast riches and inflicted unimaginable suffering on the African people. All this makes a sad story, but now we must be prepared to bury the past with its unpleasant memories and look to the future. All we ask of the former colonial powers is their good will and . . . to grant independence to the colonies in Africa. . . . It is clear that we must find an African solution to our problems, and that this can only be found in African unity. Divided we are weak. United, Africa could become one of the greatest forces for good in the world.

"Stand On Our Own"

In 1960, shortly before Nigeria gained its independence from Britain, the respected Nigerian leader Chief Obafemi Awolowo proclaimed that it was up to Nigerians to make their new country successful:

> After independence we will have to stand on our own and rely on our own resources, the unifying force, the cement . . . which had hitherto been supplied by [Britain] will be removed, and will have to be replaced by new virtues of our own which must be capable of keeping all the diverse elements of the country together, in mutual trust and harmony and with a common national purpose.

THE GUILT OF DELAY.

Congo Slave-Driver. "I'M ALL RIGHT. THEY'RE STILL TALKING."

A British cartoon criticizes the delay in outlawing slavery in the Belgian Congo

Independence at Last

At the same time that African nationalism was on the rise, many European imperialists began acknowledging that what their nations had done to Africa in the past was wrong. Increasingly large numbers of people in Europe viewed colonialism as outdated and unethical. Especially following the close of World War II, in 1945, the great powers realized that from a moral standpoint they should not and could not continue their large-scale exploitation of Africa.

One of the greatest forces in shaping new, fairer ways for these nations and peoples to treat one another was the United Nations (U.N.). This new international organization, which emerged from the chaos of World War II, recognized that an end to colonialism was both needed and inevitable. And its members instituted a transition process to prepare dependent peoples in Africa (and elsewhere) for independence. This process employed the "trust" system. Under its rules, the colonial powers were required to set target dates for granting African colonies and protectorates full independence. All of the great powers signed the U.N. Charter, one article of which states:

A 1955 photograph of the United Nations General Assembly building in New York City

Members of the United Nations which have or assume responsibilities for the administration of territories whose peoples have not yet attained a full measure of self-government recognize the principle that the interests of the inhabitants of these territories are paramount, and accept as a sacred trust the obligation to [ensure] their political, economic, social, and educational advancement, their just treatment, and their protection against abuses; to develop self-government, to take due account of the political aspirations of the peoples, and to assist them in the progressive development of their free political institutions.

In the nearly three decades that followed, almost all of the formerly unfree and exploited African peoples at last gained their independence. Listing only some of them, Libya became free of Italy in 1951; the Sudan from Britain in 1956; Ghana from Britain in 1957; the Congo from Belgium in 1960; Sierra Leone from Britain in 1961; Algeria from France in 1962; Kenya from Britain in 1962; Angola and Mozambique from Portugal in 1975; Djibouti from France in 1977; and Zimbabwe from Britain in 1980.

The Last Gasp

The mood of goodwill that accompanied the creation of so many free African nations was occasionally marred by tensions and confrontations. The worst and most famous case was the 1956 Suez Crisis, the last gasp of the old-style European imperialists in Africa.

The events leading up to the crisis began when Britain released Egypt from its protectorate status in 1922 and allowed it to form a local monarchy. Although this government ran the country's everyday affairs, behind the scenes the British

A 1956 photograph of an Egyptian warship that was placed under arrest
in Portsmouth Harbor, United Kingdom, during the Suez Crisis

remained influential, mainly because they, along with the French, wanted to maintain control over the Suez Canal.

In 1952, however, a group of Egyptian army officers led by Gamal Abdel Nasser overthrew the government. And the following year a new nation—the Republic of Egypt—formed. Nasser, who became president in 1956, took control of the canal and proclaimed it the property of Egypt—not Britain and France. Upset, the latter two nations invaded Egypt and reclaimed the canal. But then another great power, the Untied States, intervened. Upholding the spirit of the U.N.'s anti-colonial policies, U.S. leaders used their influence to force the British and French to withdraw and leave Egypt.

Nasser's Bold Stance

In 1956, faced with the onset of British and French troops into Egypt, President Nasser gave a defiant speech, saying in part:

Those who attack Egypt will never leave Egypt alive. We shall fight a regular war, a total war, a guerrilla war. Those who attack Egypt will soon realize [that] they brought disaster upon themselves. . . . But we will never submit. We shall show the world how a small country can stand in the face of great powers threatening with armed might. . . . We shall defend our freedom and independence to the last drop of our blood. This is the stanch feeling of every Egyptian. The whole Arab nation will stand by us in our common fight against aggression and domination.

The withdrawal of Britain and France from Egypt in a sense sounded the death knell for Europe's traditional exploitation of Africa. Sadly, it did not mark the end of the continent's troubles. Poverty, disease, and civil discords continued and remain serious problems today. But when modern Africans confront these ills, they do so not as powerless, hopeless dependents of domineering outside powers, but as proud, self-governing nations. Many Africans still embrace the words of the great Kwame Nkrumah, who said in 1961:

> I believe strongly and sincerely that with the deep-rooted wisdom and dignity, the innate respect for human lives, [and] the intense humanity that is our heritage, the African race . . . will emerge [as] a great power whose greatness is indestructible because it is built not on fear, envy, and suspicion, nor won at the expense of others, but founded on hope, trust, friendship and directed to the good of all mankind.

Timeline

BC

ca. 3100   Egypt establishes the world's first major nation-state.

ca. 631   Greek settlers found a colony in what is now Libya, in North Africa.

264-164   Rome defeats the North African empire of Carthage in the three Punic Wars.

AD

316   Two Greeks convert the royal family of Ethiopia to Christianity.

639-642   Muslim armies enter Egypt from the east.

1324-1326   King Mansa Musa of Mali embarks on a pilgrimage to Mecca.

1415   Portugal seizes Ceuta, a Muslim stronghold in northern Africa.

1418   The Portuguese begin settling the island of Madeira, off of Africa's northwestern coast.

1444   Portuguese navigator Dini Dias arrives at Cape Verde and the Mouth of the Senegal River, in western Africa.

1483   Portuguese ships reach the mouth of the Congo River.

1487   Portuguese navigator Bartholomew Dias reaches the Cape of Good Hope, at Africa's southern tip.

1497   Portuguese ship captain Vasco da Gama sails to what is now Kenya.

1507-1543   Reign of Nzinga Mvemba, Congolese king converted to Christianity by the Portuguese.

1530   British traders establish ties with western Africa.

1562   The British start dealing in African slaves.

1612   The Dutch build a fort on the coast of Ghana.

1652   The Dutch East India Company sets up a trading station on the coast of South Africa.

1794   Scottish explorer Mungo Park travels along the Niger River.

1798   French general Napoleon Bonaparte invades Egypt.

1807   Britain bans the African slave trade.

1834   The British abolish slavery in all of their territories.

1835-1837   The Boers trek inland to flee British rule in South Africa.

1855	Scottish explorer David Livingstone sees and names Victoria Falls.
1858	English explorer Richard Francis Burton reaches Lake Tanganyika, in eastern Africa.
1865	French-American explorer Paul du Chaillu becomes the first modern European to see African Pygmies.
1879	The British fight and defeat the Zulus in South Africa.
1880-1881	The British and Boers clash in the First Boer War.
1884-1885	The major European powers convene in Berlin to divide up the African continent.
1899-1902	The British defeat the Boers in the Second Boer War.
1908	The Belgian government strips King Leopold II's power in the Congo.
1914-1918	World War I draws in all the great powers; the biggest loser, Germany, surrenders its African colonies.
1919	Delegates from fifteen nations convene the First Pan-African Congress in Paris.
1945	The United Nations sets standards for decolonizing Africa and the world.
1956	Britain and France invade Egypt in the Suez Canal crisis.
1957	Ghana becomes independent of Britain.
1962	Algeria receives its independence from France.
1975	Portugal grants Angola its independence.

⚜ Sources

CHAPTER ONE:
Africa Before the European Onslaught

p. 12, "Western European civilization . . ." W. H. McNeill, *The Rise of the West: A History of the Human Community* (Chicago: University of Chicago Press, 1992), 707–708.

p. 14, "The entire Mediterranean Sea . . ." Naphtali Lewis, *Life in Egypt Under Roman Rule* (Oxford, England: Clarendon Press, 1983), 10.

p. 14, "from the surf-beaten ocean shores . . ." Juvenal, "Tenth Satire," in Peter Green, trans., *Juvenal: The Sixteen Satires* (New York: Penguin, 1974), 210.

p. 14, "They have no voice . . ." Pliny the Elder, "Natural History," in John F. Healy, trans., *Pliny the Elder: Natural History, A Selection* (New York: Penguin, 1991), 57.

p. 15, "The Atlas tribe is primitive . . ." Ibid.

p. 17, "[I] pursued my journey . . ." Ibn Battuta, "Travels in Asia and Africa, 1325–1354," Modern History SourceBook, Fordham University, http://www.fordham.edu/halsall/source/1354-ibnbattuta.html.

CHAPTER TWO:
The Coming of the Portuguese

p. 23, "Henry's vision and purpose . . ." A. Adu Boahen, "The Coming of the Europeans," in Alvin M. Josephy, ed., *The Horizon History of Africa* (New York: American Heritage, 1971), 307.

p. 24, "[Portugal's] position [directly in] the path . . ." Robert W. July, *A History of the African People* (Long Grove, IL: Waveland Press, 1997), 150.

p. 27, "The inhabitants of this country . . ." "Log of Vasco da Gama," Modern History SourceBook, Fordham University, http://www.fordham.edu/halsall/mod/1497degama.html.

p. 28, "Portugal, pursuing the expansionist dreams . . ." July, *A History of the African People,* 84.

p. 28, "We were still at supper . . ." "Log of Vasco da Gama."

CHAPTER THREE:
The Dutch and Other Europeans

p. 34, "[When] they came to a river . . ." Josephy, *The Horizon History of Africa,* 377.

p. 36, "It was a revolting mess . . ." Chancellor Williams, *The Destruction of Black Civilization* (Chicago: Third World Press, 1987), 253.

p. 38, "When you go into [the city] . . ." Molefi K. Asante, *The History of Africa: The Quest for Eternal Harmony* (New York: Routledge, 2007), 167.

p. 40, "Moving eastward with his herds . . ." July, *A History of the African People,* 160.

p. 42, "By [1700] there was hardly a coastal region . . ." Boahen, "The Coming of the Europeans," 326.

CHAPTER FOUR:
The Horrors of the Slave Trade

p. 44, "The European concept . . ." James Lynch, ed., *Africa's Glorious Legacy* (Richmond, VA: Time-Life, 1994), 13.

p. 45, "nothing remotely human. . ." Ibid.

p. 45, "The animal character that appears . . ." Arthur de Gobineau, "Essay on the Inequality of Human Races," in Kevin Reilly, Stephen Kaufman, and Angela Bodino, eds., *Racism: A Global Reader* (Armonk, NY: M. E. Sharp, 2003), 195.

p. 49, "Many Africans became enmeshed . . ." Williams, *The Destruction of Black Civilization,* 252.

p. 50, "would be a built-in motivation . . ." Ibid.

CHAPTER FIVE:
A New Round of European Explorers

p. 54, "slavery would shrivel and die . . ." July, *A History of the African People,* 271.

p. 54, "At first European enterprise took the form . . ." Ibid., 276.

p. 54, "The great object of your journey . . ." Christopher Hibbert, *Africa Explored: Europeans in the Dark Continent,* 1769–1889 (New York: Cooper Square, 2002), 75.

p. 56, "fired the imagination and ambition . . ." Basil Davidson, *Africa in History* (New York: Simon & Schuster, 2005), 282.

p. 57, "[At first] one sees nothing . . ." "Livingstone Discovers Victoria Falls, 1855," EyeWitness to History, http://www.eyewitnesstohistory.com/livingstone.htm.

p. 59, "Draw a thousand pounds now . . ." "Henry Morton Stanley, 1841–1904," Princeton University, http://libweb5.princeton.edu/visual_materials/maps/websites/africa/stanley/stanley.html.

p. 60, "I pushed back the crowds . . ." "Stanley Finds Livingstone, 1871," EyeWitness to History, http://www.eyewitnesstohistory.com/stanley.htm.

p. 61, "a pious Muslim . . ." Basil Davidson, *African Kingdoms* (New York: Time-Life, 1978), 172.

p. 61, "A dwarf! . . ." "Paul du Chaillu: Travels in Africa, 1868–1870," Modern History SourceBook, Fordham University, http://www.fordham.edu/halsall/mod/1870chaillu-africa.html.

CHAPTER SIX:
Europe's Mad Scramble for Africa

p. 63, "I beg to direct your attention to Africa . . ." Thomas Pakenham, *The Scramble for Africa* (New York: Random House, 1991), 1.

p. 63, "To open to civilization . . ." Adam Hochschild, *King Leopold's Ghost* (Boston: Houghton Mifflin, 1998), 44.

p. 63, "I do not want to risk . . ." Ibid., 58.

p. 65, "knit adventurers, traders, and missionaries . . ." Pakenham, *The Scramble for Africa,* 239.

p. 66, "All the powers exercising . . ." "The Berlin Conference: The General Act of Feb. 26, 1885," Professor John V. O'Brien's History Page, http://web.jjay.cuny.edu/~jobrien/reference/ob45.html.

p. 67, "gun—not trade or the cross . . ." Pakenham, *The Scramble for Africa,* xxiii.

p. 69, "We have conquered for ourselves . . ." "Kaiser Wilhelm II: A Place in the Sun, 1901," Modern History SourceBook, Fordham University, http://www.fordham.edu/halsall/mod/1901kaiser.html.

p. 71, "[I accuse you of] deceit, fraud . . ." "George Washington Williams's Open Letter to King Leopold on the Congo," Blackpast.org, Online Reference Guide by Professor Quintard Taylor, http://www.blackpast.org/?q=george-washington-williams-open-letter-king-leopold-congo-1890.

CHAPTER SEVEN:

British Imperialism in Africa

p. 75, "Take up the White Man's burden . . ." Rudyard Kipling, "The White man's Burden," Modern History SourceBook, Fordham University, http://www.fordham.edu/halsall/mod/Kipling.html.

p. 76, "To treat [the native African] kindly . . ." Roy Lewis and Yvonne Foy, *Painting Africa White: The Human Side of British Colonialism* (New York: Universe Books, 1971), 28.

p. 76, "The essential point in dealing with Africans . . ." Capt. F. D. Lugard, "The Rise of Our East African Empire," Modern History SourceBook, Fordham University, http://www.fordham.edu/halsall/mod/1893lugard.html.

p. 78, "Egypt may now almost be said . . ." Earl of Cromer, "Why Britain Acquired Egypt in 1882," Modern History SourceBook, Fordham University, http://www.fordham.edu/halsall/mod/1908cromer.html.

p. 80, "Before we knew [what was happening] . . ." Quoted in Pakenham, *The Scramble for Africa,* 68.

p. 81, "In their conflicts with black people . . ." Ibid., 45.

CHAPTER EIGHT:

Africans Throw Off the European Yoke

p. 85, "contained the germ of its own destruction . . ." July, *A History of the African People,* 516.

p. 86, "The natives of Africa must have . . ." Asante, *The History of Africa,* 262.

p. 86, "little by little . . ." Davidson, *African Kingdoms*, 331.

p. 88, "For centuries Europeans dominated . . ." Kwame Nkrumah, "I Speak of Freedom," Modern History SourceBook, Fordham University, http://www.fordham.edu/halsall/mod/1961nkrumah.html.

p. 88, "After independence we will have to stand . . ." "The Story of Africa: Independence," BBC World Service Online, http://www.bbc.co.uk/worldservice/africa/features/storyofafrica/index_section14.shtml.

p. 91, "Members of the United Nations . . ." U. N. Charter, Article 73, http://www.un.org/en/documents/charter/chapter11.shtml.

p. 94, "Those who attack Egypt . . ." President Gamal Abdel Nasser, "Denouncement of the Proposal for a Canal Users' Association," Modern History Source Book, Fordham University, http://www.fordham.edu/halsall/mod/1956Nasser-suez1.html.

p. 95, "I believe strongly . . ." Nkrumah, "I Speak of Freedom."

Bibliography

Selected Books

Asante, Molefi K. *The History of Africa: The Quest for Eternal Harmony.* New York: Routledge, 2007.

Burnside, Madeleine, and Rosemarie Robotham. *Spirit of the Passage: The Transatlantic Slave Trade in the Seventeenth Century.* New York: Simon & Schuster, 1997.

Collins, Robert O., and James M. Burns. *A History of Sub-Saharan Africa.* New York: Cambridge University Press, 2007.

Davidson, Basil. *Africa in History.* New York: Simon & Schuster, 2005.

————, ed. *African Civilization Revisited.* Trenton, NJ: Africa World Press, 1991.

Dugard, Martin. *Into Africa: The Epic Adventures of Stanley and Livingstone.* New York: Broadway, 2004.

Hibbert, Christopher. *Africa Explored: Europeans in the Dark Continent, 1769-1889.* New York: Cooper Square, 2002.

Hochschild, Adam. *King Leopold's Ghost.* Boston: Houghton Mifflin, 1998.

July, Robert W. *A History of the African People.* Long Grove, IL: Waveland Press, 1997.

Louis, W. M. Roger, ed. *The Oxford History of the British Empire. 5 vols.* New York: Oxford University Press, 1998-1999.

Oliver, Roland. *The African Experience*. London: Weidenfeld and Nicolson, 1999.

Pakenham, Thomas. *The Scramble for Africa*. New York: Random House, 1991.

Parry, J. H. *Trade and Dominion: The European Overseas Empires in the Eighteenth Century*. New York: Sterling, 2001.

Postma, Johannes. *The Atlantic Slave Trade*. Westport, CT: Greenwood Press, 2005.

Reilly, Kevin, Stephen Kaufman, and Angela Bodino, eds. *Racism: A Global Reader*. Armonk, NY: M. E. Sharp, 2003.

Reynolds, Jonathan T., and Erik Gilbert. *Africa in World History*. New York: Prentice Hall, 2003.

Williams, Chancellor. *The Destruction of Black Civilization*. Chicago: Third World Press, 1987.

Web Sites

EyeWitness to History
http://www.eyewitnesstohistory.com

Modern History SourceBook
http://www.fordham.edu/halsall/mod/modsbook.html

The Scramble for Africa
http://www.saburchill.com/history/chapters/empires/0048.html

The Story of Africa
http://www.bbc.co.uk/worldservice/specials/1624_story_of_africa/index.shtml

The Trans-Atlantic Slave Trade
http://www.slavevoyages.org/tast/index.faces

❊ Index

✲ Picture Credits

8-9:   Used under license from iStockphoto.com

13:       Used under license from iStockphoto.com

15:       Mary Evans Picture Library/Alamy

16:       North Wind Picture Archives/Alamy

18:       Used under license from iStockphoto.com

20-21:   Used under license from iStockphoto.com

25:       INTERFOTO/Alamy

26:       Daisy Images/Alamy

29:       Mary Evans Picture Library/Alamy

30:       Used under license from iStockphoto.com

37:       Used under license from iStockphoto.com

39:       imagebroker/Alamy

41:       Mary Evans Picture Library/Alamy

44:       Used under license from iStockphoto.com

47:       Pictorial Press Ltd./Alamy

51:       Lordprice Collection/Alamy

55:       The Art Archive/Alamy

58:       World History Archive/Alamy

60:       Mary Evans Picture Library/Alamy

65:       Used under license from iStockphoto.com

68:       Classic Image/Alamy

71:       Mary Evans Picture Library/Alamy

75:       Mary Evans Picture Library/Alamy

77:       North Wind Picture Archives/Alamy

79:       Used under license from iStockphoto.com

82:       INTERFOTO/Alamy

87:       PRISMA ARCHIVO/Alamy

89:       Pictorial Press Ltd./Alamy

90:       Used under license from iStockphoto.com

92:       Trinity Mirror/Mirrorpix/Alamy